IMAGES
of America

STAMFORD

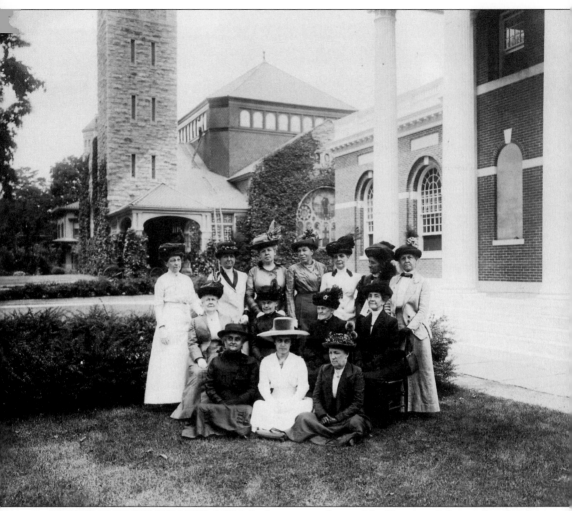

LADIES ON THE LIBRARY LAWN. Ladies pose in front of the Ferguson Library, shortly after it opened in 1911. In the background is the Presbyterian church at Broad and Summer. This is the present site of the Caldor Department Store.

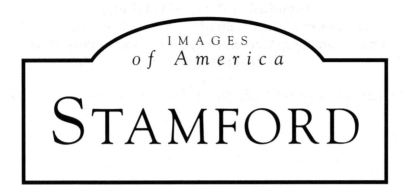

IMAGES
of America

STAMFORD

Bonnie K. Bull

ARCADIA

First published 1997
Copyright © Bonnie K. Bull, 1997

ISBN 0-7524-0859-3

Published by Arcadia Publishing,
an imprint of the Chalford Publishing Corporation,
One Washington Center, Dover, New Hampshire 03820.
Printed in Great Britain

Library of Congress Cataloging-in-Publication Data applied for

HOYT-BARNUM HOUSE. Located on Bedford Street, next to the police station, this house is now a museum of the Stamford Historical Society. The photograph shows the house as it looked in 1900, but the house was built in 1699 by Samuel Hoyt. It was later owned by the Barnum family. It is the only example of seventeenth-century architecture in Stamford and was placed on the National Register of Historic Places in 1969.

Contents

Acknowledgments

I would especially like to thank two people who are no longer living, but without whose help this book would not be possible. They are Lois Dater and Carl Lobozza. Without their efforts there would be no Photographic Collection at the Stamford Historical Society for me to draw on. Each put immeasurable time into gathering, researching, and storing the collection. Carl also contributed his photographic skills, and Lois' painstakingly small penciled notations and references on the back of each photo have been my guiding light.

I would also like to thank the living at the Stamford Historical Society: Linda Baulsir, Executive Director, for giving me complete freedom with the book and the Photographic Collection; Ron Marcus, Librarian, whose vast historical knowledge and thoroughly organized library have served me well; Karen Schoen, Curator, for listening and teaching me museum procedures; Ruth Mushkin, Office Administrator, who always greets me with a smile and an encouraging word; John Puchala, Researcher, for helping me find the answers; and Bob Rude for carrying on in the Photographic Room during my absorption with this book.

Most of all, I would like to thank my husband, Don, whose guidance and patience kept me on track.

Introduction

The photos in this book range from 1861 to 1920. On a larger scale this period spans the time between two important wars, the Civil War and the Great War, but the intention is to show what life was like in Stamford during a time of tremendous industrial and commercial expansion.

Stamford was founded in 1641, when twenty-nine men and their families left Wethersfield to settle along the Rippowam River on land purchased from Native Americans. They built a gristmill on the river near the West Main Street bridge and a meetinghouse near Veterans Park at Atlantic and Main Streets. This became the hub of their community.

The arrival of the railroad in 1848 transformed Stamford from a rural community to an industrial town with a bustling commercial center. There had been some early industry, such as Cove Mills, and the town had done a brisk trade by ocean transport, but this did not compare with the industrial opportunities afforded by the railroad and the influx of immigrant labor that followed.

The most influential industry to spring up in this fertile environment was the Yale & Towne Manufacturing Company. Established in 1868 as the Yale Lock Company, the firm began with thirty workers and grew to be a major world industry. By 1892 their factory in the South End covered 21 acres and employed 1,000 people. By 1907 they employed 3,000 people. Employment reached its peak in 1916 when 5,000 people were employed as a result of war-related contracts.

This industrial growth dramatically changed the face of Stamford. In 1871 the townspeople replaced the wooden meetinghouse with an imposing brick structure that dominated Atlantic Square, and the area where the old meetinghouse had stood became Central Park. Small frame buildings up and down Main and Atlantic Streets were replaced by two- and three-story brick "blocks" containing ground level stores with plate-glass windows displaying the latest wares. By 1900 the city had water, sewers, lights, phones, a trolley system, a public hospital, a library, and its first high school.

The train also brought Stamford closer to New York City both culturally and economically. Business opportunities opened up both ways and many wealthy New Yorkers began to summer and live in Stamford. As a result good private schools were available, yacht clubs formed, and an interest in theater developed. By the time the automobile arrived, Stamford was ripe for the advantages of quick transportation between home and work, allowing substantial real estate development to take place beyond the city limits.

It is my sincere hope that the photos in this book, selected from the archives of the Stamford Historical Society, provide the reader with a pleasant pictorial journey through one of the most significant and fascinating periods in Stamford history.

One
Streetscapes

ATLANTIC SQUARE, 1889. The focal point of downtown life was Atlantic Square. This is where the early settlers built their first meetinghouse. At left is Central Park. The large building straight ahead is the old Town Hall, erected in 1871. It stood at Atlantic and Main Streets until it burned in 1904. The rail around the park was used for tethering horses.

ATLANTIC SQUARE, 1892. The town is decorated for its 250th anniversary (celebrated one year late). The tank in the center of the square held water for the horses, until its removal in 1907. The brick building (at left) at the northwest corner of Atlantic and Main Streets was built in 1868 by Stephen Smith. The Stamford Trust Company commenced business there in 1891.

ATLANTIC STREET, 1913, looking north. Stamfordites pause to watch the Oklahoma Wild West Circus Parade. A bandwagon is just turning onto Park Row. At the head of Atlantic Street is the Ferguson Library. By this time the automobile was fast replacing the horse and buggy. The trolley at left is westbound for Port Chester.

ATLANTIC STREET, 1889. This early view shows the Town Hall and the west side of Atlantic Street opposite Central Park. The four-story building at right is the Florence Building. The hardware store on the right has a Yale key display sign over its door. Next door, the Bargain House has bins of goodies set out on the sidewalk.

UPPER ATLANTIC STREET, 1907. This photograph shows a similar view just a few years later. Looking south in the distance is the new Town Hall, built in 1905. On the west side of Atlantic Street, just to the right of center, is the Burlington Arcade Building.

CENTRAL PARK, 1905. This photograph shows the park on the left and an eastern view of Main Street all the way to St. John's Episcopal Church. Behind the park is Park Row. The bandstand, erected in 1899, was moved to Dr. Given's property in September 1907. This view is now Veterans Park and the Stamford Town Center.

CENTRAL PARK FOUNTAIN, 1871–1897. Dedicated on the Fourth of July 1871, the fountain commemorated the opening of the first water mains in Stamford by the Stamford Water Company. Water was piped from Trinity Lake, 12 miles away. The fountain was dismantled in 1897.

PARK ROW BLOCK, 1875. Completed in 1875, this building stood at the corner of Atlantic Street and Park Row, opposite the north end of Central Park. The first occupants, from left to right, were A.F. Weed & Brothers Grocers, Hubbard & Holly Dry Goods, Lockwood & Haight Apothecaries, and Haight & Holmes Dry Goods. At left, behind Park Row Block, is the Baptist church at Atlantic and Broad Streets.

SEELY'S BLOCK, *c.* 1875. This handsome structure, later known as Miller's Block, was built in 1861 by Albert Seely. It was located on Main Street between the Stamford House and the corner of Pacific Street. Tobias Bernhard, seated in the wagon on the left, established a dry goods store at this location in 1867. The upper floor housed a large meeting hall.

AERIAL VIEW, 1910, looking east from Town Hall. At far left is Central Park, with Park Row hidden behind the trees. Several trolleys pass through Atlantic Square and there are numerous tracks going in all directions. Looking up Main Street, the white building on the left with the twin towers is the Grand Union House (formerly Union House). The building on the southeast corner of Atlantic and Main Streets is the Quintard Block, erected in the spring of 1861 by Isaac Quintard. Retail establishments occupied the main floor while law and real estate offices were on the second floor. The triangular building with the domed tower is the Whitney Building on Canal Street, erected in 1891 by George E. Whitney. The decorative four-story

building to its right is the First National Bank Building. The original arched windows on the lower floors have been replaced with picture windows. Construction of this building was begun in 1872 and the gravel from the excavation was used to fill in the canal. (In 1833 the canal was dredged and opened to within 175 feet of Atlantic Square so ships could unload close to downtown. The railroad bridged it and it was gradually filled in after 1868, becoming today's Canal Street). To the right of the bank is the Lyman Hoyt Building, erected in 1884. This same view today is Veterans Park and the Stamford Town Center.

EAST SIDE OF ATLANTIC SQUARE, 1889, looking north. The building with the arched roof and bay window is the C.O. Miller Building, built in 1882. C.O. Miller was a leading dry goods merchant. The building still stands today, but only the roof line is the same. To the left is the Crystal Palace, built in 1884 by the Ayres Brothers. The Merrill Business College occupied the second floor.

THE FESSENDON BLOCK, 1892. This building, all decked out for the town's 250th anniversary, was located on the east side of Atlantic Street next to the C.O. Miller Building. At the time of this photograph its occupants were, from left to right, J.K. Lawrence & Co. Druggists, The Brunswick Dining Room, H. Sawyer Daskam Grocer, and the New York Meat Market.

BEDFORD STREET, 1889. Looking south toward Broad Street, the steeple of the Baptist church can be seen in the distance. The second house in on the left is King School and south of it is the Five Chimney House. Originally on the west side of the street and later moved, it was a warehouse for the Waring Iron Foundry.

LOWER ATLANTIC STREET, 1906, looking north. The first building on the left is St. John's R.C. Church. The spire was not completed until 1928. The spire of the Congregational church, located at Atlantic and Bank Streets, can be seen further up the street on the left. The street became quite residential as one proceeded away from Atlantic Square.

MAIN AND BANK STREETS, 1889. The red brick building with the round tower at the apex of Main and Bank Streets is the Stamford Savings Bank. It also housed the Stamford National Bank until 1905, when the latter built a six-story skyscraper next door. A Stamford landmark for many years, the "Old Red Bank" was razed in March 1969.

MINOR PLACE, c. 1880. The north side of Main Street between Atlantic and Bank Streets was known as Minor Place. The frame buildings shown were built by Simeon H. Minor around 1845. In this photograph the building at left is occupied by Samuel Price, Grocer. At right is Otto Makowsky's Barber Shop. This building was razed in 1912 to make way for the Stamford Trust Co. Building.

MAIN STREET, c. 1900. Looking west from the Town Hall, the farthest building is the Washington Building at Bank Street. The tall building, occupied by Martin Brothers, is the Irving Building. The three-story frame building housed the Metz School of Music. Telephone poles and wires dominate the scene. Phones were first introduced to Stamford in 1880.

WEST MAIN STREET BRIDGE, c. 1910. Shot from the top of Greenwood Hill, this photograph provides a view of the bridge and the city. To the left of the bridge is the Diamond Ice Co. with the Methodist church steeple rising above it. The Congregational steeple is to the right. This bridge is on the National Register of Historic Places.

SUMMER STREET, *c.* 1900. The view is looking north from North Street. Trolley tracks can be seen in the center of the road.

NORTH STREET BRIDGE, 1900. This stone bridge over the Rippowam River had just been built by John M. Ferris.

BROAD STREET, 1906. Although close to downtown, Broad Street is very residential.

BROAD STREET BRIDGE, 1900. The view is to the southwest, showing the junction of Washington Avenue with Broad and River Streets. River Street is now part of Washington Boulevard. It seems eerily quiet compared with today's heavy traffic.

OLIVER STREET BRIDGE, April 1913. This iron trussed bridge was built in 1887 by the Berlin Iron Bridge Company. The street was later renamed Pulaski Street. The bridge was recently replaced with a modern structure.

AERIAL VIEW, c. 1905, looking south. Just to the right of center is Central Park. The flagpole can be seen extending into the air. The spire on the right is the Congregational church at Atlantic and Bank Streets. The Burlington advertisement is on the Grand Opera House. Park Row Block is opposite it.

Two
Business and Industry

STARK & WILSON, c. 1890. Established by J.L. Lockwood in 1853, it was purchased in 1884 by longtime employees Stark and Wilson. The business occupied all three floors of the building located at 166 Main Street. Second from left is James Wilson, followed by Arthur R. Stark and William Stark. The firm became Stark Brothers in 1892.

STAMFORD'S FIRST BANK. This was the home of Stamford's first bank. The Stamford Bank opened in 1834 in this building, a converted grocery store located on Main Street just behind the Town Hall. In 1865 it became the Stamford National Bank. In 1886, the bank moved in with the Stamford Savings Bank at Main and Bank Streets.

P.W. SHEA GROCERIES AND FEED, c. 1905. William Patrick Shea, at center in apron, established this store at 17 West Main Street in 1902. Next to him is his wife, Mary Jane, and seated in front are their two children, William and Helen. The business was successful and required five assistants and three wagons to deliver orders.

EDWIN S. WEBB, DRY GOODS, *c.* 1894. This store was located in Minor Block, on the north side of Main Street near Atlantic Street. Standing out front are Edwin Webb and his daughter Sara, eight years old. Mr. Webb opened his business at this location in 1887.

WILBUR E. LEWIS, DRUGGIST, *c.* 1890, now 97 Atlantic Street. Mr. Lewis, in the doorway with his children, began this business in 1880. In 1890 he sold it to J.D. Goulden. It is said Lewis once sold 2,743 glasses of soda water in one day. Mr. Lewis founded Acme Bottling Works, leaving in 1890 to establish Eagle Bottling Works in Glenbrook. There he manufactured soda water.

JIM R. EELLS' CITY MARKET, *c.* 1895, Main Street, one door east of the Union House. Eells, standing just to the left of the doorway, became sole owner of the market in 1883. The man in the doorway is Frank Jessup. George, the shoeshine boy at left, was known for his juggling act.

BRADY & CHADEAYNE FURNITURE, *c.* 1888, Bell Block, Atlantic Street. Stephen S. Chadeayne (left) and Elmer E. Brady (right) started their business in 1888. Two years later they moved to 95 Atlantic Street where they also had a funeral parlor. Mrs. Chadeayne was the first licensed female mortician in Connecticut.

OTTO MAKOWSKY'S BARBER SHOP, *c.* 1893, located in Minor Block on Main Street. Otto is standing at left next to the bicycle. He moved his shop to Main Street when the building was razed to make way for the new Stamford Trust Building.

VOSKA & OTTO TAILORS, 1912, 45–47 Bank Street, Washington Block. A magazine advertisement of the same year states: "Suits and overcoats to order from $25 up. We mean of the better kinds."

THE ADVOCATE, c. 1890, Advocate Place. *The Stamford Advocate* is the oldest local business concern of continuous operation. The newspaper was established in 1829 by Albert Hanford. It was acquired in 1867 by the Gillespie family, who are shown here posing in front of the Advocate Building. In the doorway with his arms folded is Edward T.W., at right is Richard H., and at left is Richard Jr. Standing in the doorway at right is Frank Weed.

STAMFORD NEWS, 1892. This paper, which began in 1886, was published and edited by George W. Sawter. The building was located at the northeast corner of Bedford and Broad Streets until 1932, when it was replaced by the building now occupied by McDonald's Restaurant.

SILVER DOLLAR CAFE, c. 1892. This saloon opened on March 16, 1892, at 165 Main Street at Quintard Place. The owner was John H. Lee. The bar was so long it required six bartenders to attend it. The floor was inlaid with 800 silver dollars and several gold pieces. It was one of the most prosperous establishments in the community.

UNIDENTIFIED SALOON, c. 1898. The one-legged man is remembered as being a bookkeeper at Stamford Hospital. Note the brass spittoons between the bar and the footrail and the numerous paintings on the wall behind the bar.

WASHINGTON HOUSE/WEBB'S TAVERN, Bank and Clark Streets. In October 1789, George Washington stopped here for breakfast on his way to Massachusetts. Kept as a hotel by David Webb, it was renamed in honor of Washington's visit. Razed in 1868, it was replaced by the Washington Building.

UNION HOUSE, c. 1870. Located on the north side of Main Street opposite Stage Street, this hotel was designed and built by Thomas P. Dixon in 1844. It was renamed the Grand Union Hotel in 1891 and later called the Carlton Hotel. It burned in 1920. The Stamford Post Office occupied the small frame building at left from 1861 until May 21, 1883.

STAMFORD HOUSE, *c.* 1915, Main and Stage Streets. First known as the Stage House, it was one of the principal stopping places for travelers between New York and Boston. Stage coaches were kept in the stage yard behind the hotel on Stage Street. To the left of the hotel is Faucett's Harness shop.

CONCERT HALL, *c.* 1891. This building stood at the northeast corner of Main and Gay Streets. It was designed and built by Thomas P. Dixon in 1850. There were stores on the street level and a large concert hall on the third floor.

ZIPF'S HOTEL AND REILLY & BOUNTY, *c.* 1887. Situated on the northwest corner of Atlantic and Cottage Place, Zipf's was built in 1886 as a summer resort. It had a large dance pavilion and the grounds were rented by local organizations for picnics. It burned in 1889. Reilly & Bounty Stonecutters was established in 1881. The firm became A.E. Bounty in 1892 when Reilly died.

JAMES H. BEDELL DAIRY, *c.* 1910. This dairy was located at 31 Oak Street.

DIAMOND ICE CO. WAGON, *c.* 1916, on Walton Place in front of the Congregational church. The Diamond Ice Co. was established in 1897 on the site of the old Woolen Mill near the West Main Street bridge. Ice was cut from the Mill Pond of the Rippowam River and eighteen to twenty wagons were used in its delivery. After 1916 only artificial ice was sold.

BOYD BROS. GRAVES & STRANG, INC., *c.* 1920. Their 1916 advertisement states: "We sell Lehigh Valley Anthracite 'The coal that Satisfies.'" The coal yard was located at 556 Canal Street, and their uptown office was F.M. West, Atlantic Street.

STAMFORD MANUFACTURING CO., *c.* 1892. Henry J. Sanford established this company in 1844 on the site of the old Holly gristmill at the Cove. The company imported tropical woods from South America and ground extracts used for dyes, drugs, and licorice paste. The company was destroyed by fire in 1919. This is the site of today's Cove Island Park.

THE COVE, *c.* 1900. Sitting on the dock is Charles Chavalle, a superintendent at the mills. A large volume of water-borne freight was handled annually by the Cove Transportation Co., which had a fleet of five or six vessels exclusively in the service of the Stamford Mfg. Co.

HARDING-SMITH WOOLEN MILL. This mill was located on the Mill River near the West Main Street bridge from 1867 to 1886. It was later occupied by the Diamond Ice Co. The building was razed in 1965 for new construction.

THE STAMFORD FOUNDRY CO., *c.* 1895, Canal Street. The foundry manufactured cast-iron stoves. Founded in 1830, the company moved several times before finally settling on Canal Street in 1851. By 1895 it covered 2 acres and employed approximately 100 men. The company closed in 1954 due to competition from more advanced electric stoves and ovens.

YALE LOCK MANUFACTURING CO., 1876. This company opened in 1869 with less than thirty persons. It was started by Linus Yale Jr. and Henry R. Towne. The name was changed to Yale & Towne Mfg. Co. in 1883. Yale, who died before the company opened, had designed bank locks and a new flat keyed lock.

YALE & TOWNE GRADUATING CLASS, 1915. Yale & Towne also ran an apprentice school. In the front row, wearing a hat and holding his overcoat, is Henry Towne. Behind the front row are the young male graduates. After graduating they will earn $3 per week. Henry Towne was president until 1915, and chairman of the board until his death in 1924.

YALE & TOWNE PACKING DEPT., Sept. 12, 1902. Employees of the department were Bessie Irvine Taff, Emily Winslow Vosburgh, Ellen Mitchell Raines, Margaret Ahern, Cora Kriger, Ella McGee, Elizabeth Jackson, Bessie Sounder, and Samuel Palmer.

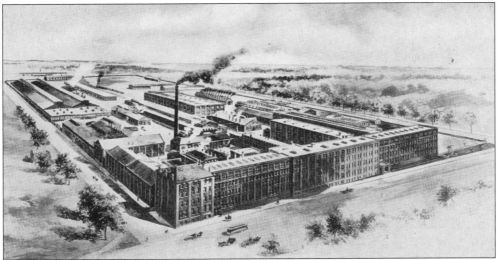

YALE & TOWNE MANUFACTURING CO., c. 1907. By 1907 the company employed 3,000 people and occupied 21 acres (the area between Pacific Street and the canal, and Market Avenue and Henry Street). Stamford became known as the Lock City. In 1959 the company closed completely in Stamford, finding more alluring business conditions elsewhere.

THE GETMAN & JUDD CO. Established in 1853 as a planing mill and lumber yard by Richard Fox and John St. John on Broad Street, it moved to the site pictured on the canal in 1877. It underwent several name changes until the above name was adopted in 1900.

GETMAN & JUDD OFFICE INTERIOR, *c*. 1898. Frank Bogardus is at left in the inner office, Fred Thompson is in the middle. In 1928, Bogardus was elected president. Fred Thompson joined the firm in 1889 and was later made secretary.

"THE TERRACE," *c.* 1895, Bedford Street. This is the residence of George Blickensderfer. In 1892 in a small shop at the back of this house, Blickensderfer invented a portable typewriter with the type set on a revolving, interchangeable cylinder. A factory was subsequently built on Atlantic Street, just below the railroad bridge. The plant closed soon after the inventor's death in 1917.

STOLLWERCK'S FACTORY, *c.* 1907. The Stollwerck Brothers Chocolate Factory was built in 1906 on Southfield Avenue. The parent company was in Cologne, Germany. After World War I, the owners returned to Germany and the factory remained vacant until Petro took it over in 1929.

ATLANTIC INSULATED WIRE AND CABLE CO., 1907. This company began operation in Stamford in 1903 in leased premises on Pacific Street. The above factory was built on Ludlow Street in 1906. The company made cable for interior, underground, and submarine use.

UNIVERSAL STAMPING MACHINE, c. 1917. Later Pitney Bowes, this early factory was located at Walnut and Pacific Streets. In 1919 Walter Bowes merged his postage stamping firm with the Chicago postage meter company of Arthur Pitney. Pitney Bowes became Stamford's most influential employer after Yale & Towne.

Three
In the Public Interest

TOWN HALL, c. 1875. This impressive brick and stone structure stood at the corner of Atlantic and Main Streets from 1871 to 1904. It was a welcome replacement for the old wooden structure the town had built in 1830 at the center of Atlantic Square. Next to it is the Congregational church at Atlantic and Bank Streets.

TOWN HALL, 1892. The Town Hall is decorated for the city's 250th anniversary. The entrance to the Town Hall was on the south side facing the Congregational church. The Town Clerk's Office can be seen just to the right of the entrance. At street level were shops, while the second story contained private and municipal offices. On the third floor was an auditorium.

TOWN HALL FIRE, 1904. One of the most disastrous fires in the history of Stamford was the burning of the Town Hall. The fire began at 7 pm on February 4, on the second floor. By 4 am the building was completely gutted.

LAYING THE CORNERSTONE, Sept. 27, 1905. After much debate it was decided to build the new Town Hall on the same site the old Town Hall had occupied. The event was well attended. The view is from Bank Street looking northwest toward Main Street.

THE NEW TOWN HALL, 1907. The new Town Hall was a fireproof Beaux Arts structure. It housed municipal offices, a police headquarters, and a jail. This building has been vacant since 1987, when the city relocated to the GTE Building at Washington and Tresser Boulevards.

TOWN LEADERS, *c*. 1913. From left to right are Mayor of Stamford Walter G. Austin, 1913–1915; Chief of Stamford Fire Department Harry W. Parker, 1903–1920; and Chief of Stamford Police Department William H. Brennan, 1905–1923.

THE 275th ANNIVERSARY CELEBRATION, 1916. As in 1892, the town went all out for the centennial celebration, decorating the buildings with buntings and flags and holding a grand parade. A large number of people gathered in the square and on the steps of the Town Hall.

STAMFORD FIRE DEPARTMENT, *c.* 1895. Seated is George Bowman, fire chief from 1887 to 1903. The Stamford Fire Department, operating out of the Luther Street Station, was organized in 1885 from several volunteer companies to a part-paid and part-call force. It began with a steam fire engine, a hose carriage, and a small ladder truck.

AMERICAN LA FRANCE STEAMER, Town Hall fire, 1904. This fire-fighting apparatus was purchased April 1892. The town was proud of its new steamer, but it did not save the Town Hall from destruction. Loss of the Town Hall was blamed on a lack of water pressure and the fact that no horses were readily available to bring up the equipment.

LOCOMOBILE at the Central Fire Station, Luther Street. The Locomobile was a combination chemical and hose car purchased on May 9, 1910. It was the department's first motorized unit. Showing it off are Chief Speh, M. Clark (seated), Lonergan, Schneider (at rear), and Mullens.

SOUTH END FIRE STATION, c. 1918. Engine & Hose Co. #2 opened formally on March 29, 1900. It was located at the southeast corner of Pacific and Henry Streets, next to Yale & Towne. Driving is Art Kelly and on the right is Victor Veit.

THE CENTRAL FIRE STATION, 1916. The fire department poses in front of the new Central Fire Station on Main Street, completed in 1915. By now the fire department was completely motorized.

AERIAL LADDER TRUCK, 1916. The fire department shows off the new Hook & Ladder apparatus out of Central Station at the 275th Anniversary Parade. The view is of Atlantic Square, looking east.

FIRST UNIFORMED POLICE OF STAMFORD, 1894. The first uniforms were purchased by Mr. W.H. Jones of Jones Drug Store. From left to right are: (front row) Dr. Francis Rogers, William H. Jones, and Edward J. Tupper; (back row) Edgar M. Toms, Richard Armstrong, Edward O'Brien, Andrew Morris, A. Lincoln Clarke, and Daniel Hickey Jr.

BICYCLE POLICEMEN. From left to right are John B. Brennan, Arnold Kurth, and Hugh Grogan. Arnold Kurth became Stamford's first bicycle policeman in 1892. He was known as the Boy Cop and wore Police Badge #1 until his retirement in 1921. John B. Brennan became police chief in 1926.

POLICE DEPARTMENT ON PARADE, 1916. The Stamford Police Department marches in the 275th Anniversary Parade on Atlantic Street. In the lead is Police Chief William H. Brennan. He was police chief from 1905 to 1923 and acting chief from 1903 to 1905.

STAMFORD POLICE DEPARTMENT PERSONNEL, 1918. Members of the police department and city officials pose in front of the Town Hall. Mayor John Treat is seated at center. He was mayor from 1916 to 1922.

POST OFFICE EMPLOYEES, *c.* 1884. The Stamford Post Office had only four employees in 1884. The post office, which had been in a frame building on Main Street next to the Union House, moved into the Town Hall in 1883.

POSTAL EMPLOYEES, 1913. The man with his hat on his knee is Postmaster Nelson Jessup (1908–1913). Seated on his left is John Bohl, postmaster from 1913 to 1921. The men are posed outside the Burlington Arcade on Atlantic Street. The post office relocated here after the Town Hall fire in 1904.

STAMFORD POST OFFICE. The Stamford Postal Service finally moved into its own building at Atlantic and Federal Streets in December 1916. The cornerstone was laid by Mayor Brown July 1915. This is today's Atlantic Street Post Office. The entrance area was built around the two existing trees.

GLENBROOK POST OFFICE, *c.* 1900. At left is Minnie Slauson, postmistress of the Glenbrook Post Office on Courtland Avenue. Luisa Zwart, standing at right, ran a grocery business in the same building.

THE FERGUSON LIBRARY READING ROOM, April 1899. Shown is the reading room of Stamford's first library. It opened in 1882 on the second floor of the Payne Building at Atlantic and Luther Streets as a result of a bequest of $10,000 from John Day Ferguson. The townspeople raised an additional $25,000 as stipulated in the bequest.

SECOND HOME OF THE FERGUSON LIBRARY, *c*. 1908. This was the former Leeds home on Atlantic Street opposite St. John's R.C. Church. The library remained there until a new library was completed in 1911. Books were free to all to use in the reading room. Taking them away required a ticket which cost $1.50 per year.

THE FERGUSON LIBRARY, *c*. 1918. A new library was built in 1911 at the head of Atlantic Street. It was built on the site of the Gothic House at the corner of Broad and Bedford Streets. Expanded in 1930 and again in 1982, the same Georgian facade looks out over Atlantic Street today.

STAMFORD'S FIRST HOSPITAL, *c.* 1900. Stamford's first hospital opened in 1896 in a Victorian mansion called Rothenfels. It was located on E. Main Street at the foot of Noroton Hill. The hospital opened with thirty metal beds (all painted white), and four visiting and two consulting doctors.

JUDGE JOHN CLASON AND HIS OXEN TEAM. The purchase of the first hospital was made possible by the initial donation of $43,000 by a sixty-five-year-old bachelor who led a simple life, but had been a probate judge for many years. A state grant of $25,000 and donations of other Stamford citizens brought the total start-up fund to $100,000.

STAMFORD HOSPITAL, 1913. The first main building of the present Stamford Hospital on Broad Street was opened on September 20, 1913. The new, 100-bed, brick hospital cost $400,000.

DR. FRANCIS ROGERS, c. 1900. The doctor is posed outside his home on Atlantic Street at the corner of Cottage Street. He served eleven years on the Board of School Visitors and was the town health officer for five years.

THE YMCA, c. 1890. The YMCA was established in Stamford in 1882. Its purpose was to provide social activities for respectable men of small means. This building was located on the west side of Atlantic near Broad. The garage at rear was a gymnasium. By 1892 it had grown to 370 members.

THE YMCA, c. 1918. The YMCA soon outgrew the house on upper Atlantic Street and, in 1908, built a new brick building further south on Atlantic Street next to the post office (which was built in 1916). A wing at the back housed a swimming pool and a gymnasium.

Four
The Learning Curve

CATHERINE AIKEN SCHOOL FOR GIRLS, *c.* 1880. This private girls school was founded in 1855 as the Stamford Female Seminary. From 1860 to 1880, it was located in the building shown above on Glenbrook Road. It then relocated to Bedford Street where the Congregational church now stands.

KING SCHOOL FOR BOYS, *c*. 1914, Bedford Street. This private boys school, still in operation today, was established in 1876 by Hiram U. King. The school moved to Bedford Street in 1878 where it remained for the next fifty years. It also occupied a smaller one-story building on Bedford Street.

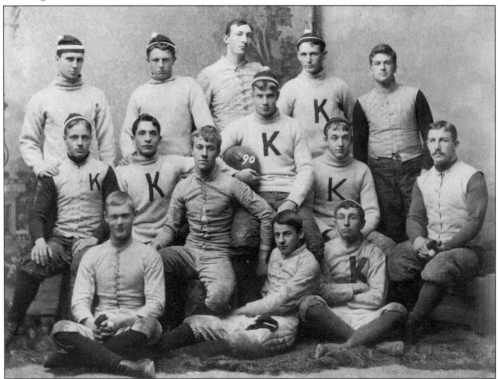

THE H.U. KING FOOTBALL TEAM, 1890. Football was a popular school sport in the late 1800s. Schools played one another at scheduled events much as they do today and the importance of team sports for building good character was stressed.

LOW-HEYWOOD SCHOOL, *c.* 1905. This school, founded in 1883, was housed in the old Ferguson Mansion on Atlantic Street at the time of this picture. The property was later taken for the new post office. Low-Heywood School for girls still operates today on Newfield Avenue in conjunction with King School.

STAMFORD ACADEMY, *c.* 1909. This boys military school was located on Lawn Avenue.

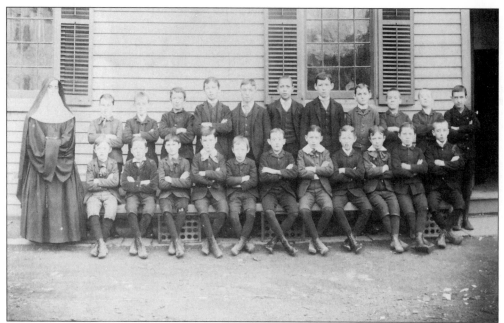

ST. JOHN'S CATHOLIC SCHOOL, *c.* 1885, Meadow (later Hawthorne) Street. In 1876, the old St. John's Church was converted into a school and the Sisters of Mercy from Hartford were placed in charge. In 1906 a new school was built on Bell Street behind the Atlantic Street Church.

STAMFORD HIGH SCHOOL, 1916. Burdick Middle School on Forest Street, now vacant, served as Stamford's high school from 1896 until the present high school on Strawberry Hill was built in 1928. It was later renamed Burdick in honor of Oscar L. Burdick, the first assistant superintendent.

STATE CHAMPIONS, 1910. The Stamford High School football team won the state championship in 1910. The team enjoyed several successful seasons under the leadership of Michael A. Boyle, who became head coach in 1907. The team won the national championship in 1920.

BASKETBALL CHAMPS, 1904. The Stamford High girls basketball team won the state championship in 1904.

HENRY STREET SCHOOL, *c.* 1900. This school stood on the south side of Henry Street between Atlantic and Pacific Streets. It was built around 1880 and demolished in 1921. While the architecture is quite charming, most of the old wooden schools of the time were being replaced by brick structures.

WEST STAMFORD SCHOOL, *c.* 1900. This school was located on West Main Street in the Richmond Hill section.

ELM STREET SCHOOL, c. 1900. By 1891 there were 2,595 pupils in Stamford schools. The schools were filling to overflowing faster than the town could build them.

WILLIAM STREET SCHOOL, 1892. This school was built in 1890. The teacher on the right is Miss Ericson. Charles Toms is in the third row, third from right, and Ed Scofield is in the first row on the right.

GLENBROOK SCHOOL, *c.* 1907. Glenbrook received a new four-room schoolhouse on Crescent Street in 1898. Later, a second story was added.

GLENBROOK SCHOOL, *c.* 1900. The teacher standing at rear on the right is Clara Trowbridge.

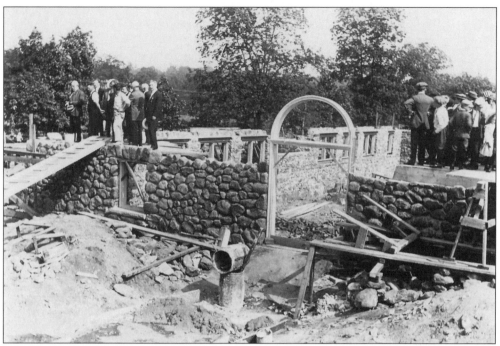

WILLARD SCHOOL, 1913. The foundation is being laid for the new consolidated school on High Ridge Road. The pupils of the High Ridge, North Stamford, Roxbury, and Turn of River one-room schools were transferred here when it opened in 1914. The school was later renamed Martha Hoyt. It is now the home of the Stamford Historical Society.

WILLARD SCHOOL, HIGH RIDGE ROAD, c. 1918. Standing in the third row, third from right is Mrs. Martha Hoyt. In 1940 the school was renamed Martha Hoyt in honor of its principal, who retired in 1933 at the age of seventy. A school on the north side of Vine Road was built and dedicated as Willard School in 1940.

BANGALL SCHOOL, *c.* 1907. Mrs. Sara Stevens is pictured with her class. Bangall School was the last of the one-room schools to close in 1949. Located at Westover and Roxbury Roads, it now forms part of the Friends' Meeting House.

MAYAPPLE ROAD SCHOOLHOUSE, early 1900s. The teacher is Minnie Slauson and two of the students are Cortland Jones and Earl Waters.

Five

Sacred Places

PRESBYTERIAN CHURCH, *c.* 1900, Broad and Summer Streets. The Presbyterian Society was incorporated in Stamford in 1853. Their first church was struck by lighting and burned in 1882. They built the Italian Renaissance structure pictured above to replace it. This church was completed in 1884 and stood next to the Ferguson Library until 1957.

CONGREGATIONAL CHURCH, *c.* 1900. This was the fifth edifice of the Congregationalists, which was the denomination of the first settlers. Built in 1858, it stood on the southwest corner of Atlantic and Bank Streets, until it was razed in 1911. It was replaced by the Citizens Savings Bank and a new church was built on Bedford Street.

CONGREGATIONAL CHURCH INTERIOR, *c.* 1890. This is the interior of the church at Atlantic and Bank Streets. The altar sign proclaims, "Christ Is Risen" and the altar plants are palms, suggesting it is Easter time. The church was designed by Gage Inslee.

REVEREND SAMUEL SCOVILLE, *c.* 1890. Samuel Scoville was the pastor of the Congregational Church from 1879 to 1899. He is best remembered for his crusade against intemperance and his efforts to alleviate poverty during the depression of the 1880s.

METHODIST CHURCH, *c.* 1905. The Methodist church was located at River (now Washington Boulevard) and Main Streets at the end of West Park (now Columbus Park). It was located there from 1859 to 1959.

BAPTIST CHURCH, *c.* 1907. This church was located at Broad and Atlantic Streets from 1860 to 1954, now the location of Landmark Square. The Baptist church was founded in Stamford in 1773.

ST. JOHN'S R.C. CHURCH AND RECTORY, *c.* 1905, Atlantic Street. Built of gray stone quarried locally, the church was dedicated in 1886. The spire was not completed until 1928. St. John's is the Mother Church to Stamford's seven Catholic parishes. The rectory, built in 1850, was acquired by the church in 1875.

70

The Polish R. C. Church,
Stamford, Conn.

HOLY NAME OF JESUS R.C. CHURCH, 1905. In 1903 the Catholic Diocese allowed the Polish residents of Stamford to have their own parish. Shown is their first church, a clapboard building built early in 1905. It stood at the corner of South (now Washington Boulevard) and Atlantic Streets. It included a convent and parochial school.

FIRST POLISH BAND, c. 1909. The White Eagle Band was organized in 1908 under the directorship of Prof. Rudolph Svec. They are posed in front of the Polish Church. At center is Father Ignacy Kruszynski, second pastor of the church. The band later received marching uniforms.

ST. JOHN'S EPISCOPAL CHURCH, *c.* 1898. Located on Main Street, it is their third and present edifice. The church opened for services in 1891. The chapel (built 1871) and the rectory (built 1884) were built earlier before the second church burned in 1890.

UNIVERSALIST-UNITARIAN CHURCH, before 1880. This church, located at Prospect and Forest Streets, looks much the same today as it did when it was built, but everything around it has changed. The cornerstone was laid in 1870 and the parsonage, which does not appear in this picture, was built in 1880.

GLENBROOK CHAPEL, c. 1890. The chapel was built in 1885. It was intended to be a non-denominational "Sabbath School," but was under the jurisdiction of the Congregational Church. It is now Union Memorial Church. It was built at the corner of New Hope and Cottage Avenue.

WATERSIDE CHAPEL, 1901. It was organized as a "Sabbath School" in 1873. In 1901 the left wing was added. At that time the name was changed to Curtis R. Marvin Memorial Chapel in memory of the man who had organized the first chapel.

CHRISTIAN SCIENCE CHURCH, c. 1912. This denomination was formally established in Stamford in 1906. Property for a church was purchased on Prospect Street in 1907 and work began on the foundation in 1911. The church was not dedicated until 1921. Christian Science churches are not dedicated until all indebtedness is completely paid.

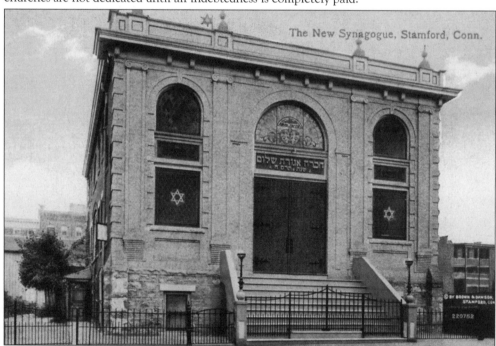

CONGREGATION AGUDATH SHOLOM, c. 1908. Incorporated in 1889, Agudath Sholom was the first organized Jewish body in Stamford. The cornerstone of this synagogue on Greyrock Place was laid on 1904. When it was destroyed by fire in 1932, a new synagogue was erected on Grove Street.

Six

The War Years

KEARSAGE GUN MEMORIAL, *c.* 1901. This cannon was placed in West Park (now Columbus) on Memorial Day 1901, in honor of Civil War soldiers. The cannon was cast at West Point in 1827, and served on the U.S.S. *Lancaster* and the U.S.S. *Kearsage*. It was removed for scrap by Luders Marine Construction Company in 1942.

CAPTAIN C.A. HOBBIE, CO. B, *c*. 1861. Charles A. Hobbie (not yet a captain at the time of the photograph) was one of six brothers who fought in the Civil War. The local post of the Grand Army of the Republic, organized in 1881, was named Hobbie Post in honor of his family. More than 500 Stamford residents served in the Union Army. Of that number, 122 died.

ARNOLD KURTH, SPANISH-AMERICAN WAR, 1898. Many men from Stamford volunteered for the cause, but most never saw action due to the large number of volunteers and the short duration of the war. The photograph shown is a New York studio portrait.

CAPTAIN GILBERT L. FITCH, 1896. Captain Fitch was with Co. C 4th Regiment of the Connecticut National Guard. During the time of the Spanish-American War, he served as major in the 3rd Regiment of the CNG. In 1930 he became brigadier general, CNG.

STATE ARMORY, c. 1912. Shown above is the new armory built by the state on South Street (now Washington Boulevard) near the railroad. It was dedicated by Governor Baldwin on Oct. 30, 1911. The Alhambra Theater moved into the old Armory, built in 1884, on River Street.

SUPER "X" 2-CYLINDER COLT MACHINE GUN, *c.* 1916. Manning the machine gun is Charles Dour, a Stamford native. The storage box reads, "Excelsior Agency, Stamford, Conn., 476 Main St., Tel. 518." The logo is an "X" over a cross which reads, "Excelsior Autocycle."

EMPLOYEES AT LUDERS BOATYARD, 1916–1919. During World War I Luders Marine Construction Company at Waterside built submarine chasers. Many factories in Stamford were given war contracts and, due to the labor shortage, men were brought in from other parts of the country.

BORGLAND, World War I. The large estate on Wire Mill Road, belonging to Gutzon Borglum (sculptor of Mt. Rushmore) and his wife, was known as Borgland. In 1918, the Borglums established a military camp on their property for Czechoslovak-American recruits waiting to be sent to France.

BATTERY F, World War I, 1917. Shown is a contingent of Battery F on Oaklawn Avenue in Stamford. After service in the Mexican War, Battery F was sent to England in September 1917. They subsequently saw action at Ostelt, France, Chateau Thiery, and the second Battle of the Marne.

BATTERY F, World War I, 1917. Men from Stamford at Fort Devens, Massachusetts, make themselves presentable.

THE BOYS COME HOME, 1919. Returning World War I soldiers were met at the freight yards by city officials. At the center is Mayor John Treat, to his left is Police Chief William H. Brennan, and to his right is Fire Chief Harry Parker.

VETERANS OF BATTERY F ON PARADE, 1919. Returning veterans parade on Main Street at Grove.

WILLARD SCHOOL, 1919. Soldiers from North Stamford, which was outside the city limits, were welcomed home at Willard School on August 29, 1919. Later a bronze plaque was placed on the school's front lawn in memory of those who served in World War I from "Rural Stamford."

SOLDIERS AND SAILORS MONUMENT, dedicated May 31, 1923. This monument, placed in St. John's Park at Tresser Boulevard and Main Street, names all the Stamford residents who served in World War I and all prior wars of American involvement.

Seven

Down by the Shore

STAMFORD HARBOR, *c.* 1907, view of the East Channel. Ships coming into the harbor could go into Waterside at the mouth of the Mill River, or into the East Channel, which was the canal. In 1833 the canal was open to within 175 feet of Atlantic Square. Bridged by the railroad in 1848, it was rendered obsolete. After 1868 it was gradually filled in.

STAMFORD LIGHTHOUSE, 1888. This photograph shows the lighthouse during the Blizzard of '88. In 1886, Stamford received funds from Congress to dredge the harbor and work began on April 13, 1887.

SHADY SIDE, c. 1890. The *Shady Side* began daily passenger trips between Stamford and New York City in 1886. She was owned by the North and East River Transportation Co. of New York, which bought out The Stamford Transportation Co. in 1886. The latter had been carrying freight and passengers between the two cities since 1852.

THE *WARWICK*, *c.* 1892. This view shows another steamship, the *Warwick*, dropping off and picking up passengers. After the canal was widened in 1868, steamboats landed at the Canal Docks. The old steamboat dock was at Knapp's Dock at Waterside, a natural harbor at the mouth of the Mill River.

SIDE WHEELER *CETUS*, *c.* 1901. This ship, docked at Waterside, was owned by the Iron Steamboat Co.

SHIPPAN POINT HOTEL, *c.* 1900. This panoramic view shows the east shore of Shippan Point. The hotel is the building with the flag on top. Originally the Ocean House and later the

SHIPPAN SHORE, *c.* 1912. A young man seated on a large rock looks out on the Sound from the Shippan shore. In the distance is the residence of James S. Herrman on Ocean Drive East.

Shippan House, it was built in 1870. To the right is a two-story gazebo where guests could lounge or read. To the left on the shore, hidden by the trees, is a large casino or bath house.

WRECK OF ENNIS' PATENT SWIMMING BATHS, October 1894. John Ennis, builder of St. John's R.C. Church, also designed and built swimming baths at the tip of Shippan Point in the late 1880s. Here the tides could be controlled and an overhead trolley with a cord sustained the novice swimmer.

SILVER BEACH, c. 1889. Swimmers enjoy the water in front of the cottages at Shippan Point. The Gillespies of the *Advocate* owned cottages here.

COTTAGES AT SHIPPAN POINT, c. 1905. In the late 1880s several parcels of land were sold off and developed at the shore on Shippan Point. Large homes were built on the eastern shore, south of the hotel. Smaller parcels were sold along the western shore near the Yacht Club and several summer cottages were erected there at Silver Beach.

HALLOWEEN PARK, *c.* 1906.
Finch family members test the
waters. Halloween Park was
acquired by the city on
Halloween night in 1906 when
Mayor Homer Cummings broke
the tie vote. It was later renamed
Cummings Park. The land had
been salt marshes which were
filled in by pumping sand up into
them, an action which also rid
the area of its mosquito problem.

THE LAGOON AT HALLOWEEN PARK, *c.* 1907. In 1927 Jaegger's Creek was dredged,
allowing boats to enter the lagoon. It is now used as a safe harbor for boats.

STAMFORD YACHT CLUB, *c.* 1900. The yacht club formally opened July 25, 1891. It was located on the west side of Shippan Point. In addition to yachting, the club also offered a stable, two tennis courts, croquet, a restaurant, bath houses, and a dock. The building shown burned in 1913.

STAMFORD YACHT CLUB, 1914. After the first clubhouse burned in 1913, a new and larger clubhouse was built in 1914 at the same location on Ocean Drive West. The club looks much the same today as it does here.

STAMFORD YACHT CLUB PORCH, *c.* 1915. The new clubhouse had a long front porch quite suitable for summer dining. Here we see a large gathering of ladies enjoying their meal on the porch.

PONUS YACHT CLUB, *c.* 1911. This yacht club, still in existence today at the same location, was at the foot of South Street (now Washington Blvd.) at the mouth of the Mill River. The ladies, dressed in long white skirts, are out for a turn on the boat.

OUT FOR A SAIL, May 31, 1915. The only person identified in the photograph is Flora Downing, who is at top, left of the mast. Flora, a school secretary, took several professional quality parade pictures in 1913, which are part of the Stamford Historical Society Collection.

GROUP ROSIE "D," April 1910. This group looks like any group of men in any era, down at the boat for a bit of recreation.

CHRISTABEL. This attractive yacht was owned by Walton Ferguson from 1903 to 1916.

THE YACHT OF CHARLES E. HOBBIE, *c.* 1900. This almost looks like an unofficial town meeting. The man in the center in the white hat is Homer Cummings, for whom Cummings Park was named. He was the mayor of Stamford from 1900 to 1902 and again from 1904 to 1906.

COVE POND, *c.* 1900. The sign on the little garage at far left says, "Geo. E. Hobbie Plumbing & Tinning." This would be today's Weed Avenue. At the time it would have been quite close to the Stamford Manufacturing Co. on Cove Island, which burned in 1919.

MILLER'S HALF WAY HOUSE, *c.* 1900. Jacob Miller established a tavern at this location in 1876 on the Boston Post Road. Also shown is Miller's Bridge on the Noroton River at Cove Pond. Today the building is Giovanni's II Restaurant.

Eight
As the Wheel Turns

HORSE AND BUGGY OF WILBUR LEWIS, *c.* 1890. Shown in the buggy are Wilbur Lewis and his family. They have posed for a photograph outside the Wilbur Lewis home at 28 Crescent Street, Glenbrook. Mr. Lewis owned a drug store in town and then established Eagle Bottling Works in Glenbrook.

EAGLE BICYCLE. In 1883 Leonard B. Gaylor patented his design for this high wheel safety bicycle. In 1888 the Eagle Bicycle Manufacturing Company was incorporated in Stamford. Gaylor's unique design placed the small wheel in the front, making the bicycle more controllable and faster. The bike was made until 1892.

VITO SUMMA, c. 1910. The English safety bicycle, created in 1885, with two wheels of the same size, driven by a chain sprocket combination, soon surpassed the high wheel bicycle in popularity. The bicycle proved to be a simple and efficient alternative to the horse for "around town" transportation.

STANLEY STEAMER, *c.* 1900. Again we see Wilbur Lewis outside his Crescent Street home, except now there is a car in the driveway instead of a horse and buggy. Unfortunately, there is not too much room for his family. The Stanley Steamer was one of the first automobiles to appear in Stamford.

WILBUR LEWIS AT THE WHEEL, *c.* 1910. Wilbur has a new car again only this time the carriage looks more like the horse and buggy seen at the beginning of this chapter. Now there is room to take the wife and kids out for a Sunday drive.

A 1904 CADILLAC. The Mechaley Brothers, John and Joe, owned a garage at this Summer Street location from 1898 to 1923, where they sold and repaired automobiles. They first established their business in Stamford in 1891.

ROCK CRUSHER, 1914. Stamford solved the problem of making good roads economically by grinding up unwanted stone walls donated by the townspeople. Pictured above is Selectman William R. Michaels standing before the portable rock crusher purchased by the town in 1909. It was through his expertise that the whole idea came about.

STAMFORD STREET RAILROAD CAR, *c.* 1890. The first horsecar run in Stamford was in 1887 and the fare was 5¢. The original company, the Stamford Horse Railroad, was purchased by the Stamford Street Railroad in 1888. The system was electrified in 1894.

ATLANTIC SQUARE, *c.* 1902. All trolley lines were accessible from Atlantic Square. The trolley at left going south on Atlantic Street is headed for the railroad station. The car going north on Atlantic is on its way to Summer Street. The car at right is traveling east on Main Street.

ATLANTIC SQUARE, 1903. This photograph shows an open summer trolley bound for Shippan. The other trolley is headed for the Cove. The open car was purchased from the Norwalk Tramway Co.

COVE ROAD CAR NUMBER 21, 1903. The Cove Road car is changing ends on Atlantic Street at Bank Street. The Cove Road line was put into operation October 16, 1896. The cars left the Town Hall on the hour and half hour and the Cove at 15 minutes before and past the hour.

McFADDEN EXPRESS CO. TRUCK, April 1913. This is the first truck of this company. The photograph was taken in the area of the Trolley Express headquarters at Manhattan and Pacific Streets. The company handled Trolley Express freight deliveries. A car leaving New Haven at 10 am arrived in Stamford at about 4 pm. Its freight was then unloaded and delivered.

SUMMER STREET LINE, 1918. Two older four-wheeled cars face north (toward Bull's Head) at the end of Summer Street. On the right is Michael Sikora; it was his first day as a conductor.

TROLLEY CAR BARN, *c.* 1904. The trolley car barn was located at Liberty Place, later called Woodside Street. The barn was built in 1886, and was designed to accommodate ten cars and forty horses. Administrative offices and storage space were on the second floor. The building collapsed during a windstorm in 1910.

TROLLEY CAR OFFICE, *c.* 1900. The office was located between Manhattan and South Streets.

STAMFORD RAILROAD STATION, built 1867. The first train arrived in Stamford on December 25, 1848. When the New York to New Haven line was completed in January 1849, trains ran on a daily basis. The station shown was a long brick building that stood between the east and westbound tracks just east of Atlantic Street.

THE NEW FOUR-TRACK SYSTEM, 1898. This photograph was taken looking north over the New Haven tracks from Getman & Judd at Canal Street. In the mid-1890s the system was changed from two to four tracks. At this time most of the road crossings were elevated and bridged.

THE NEW RAILROAD STATION, *c.* 1905. When the new four-track system was installed in the 1890s, the road crossings were elevated and bridged, making the old station below the new grade level. This necessitated razing the old station and building a new one.

ENGINE NO. 836, *c.* 1906. This photograph shows a locomotive pulling into the South Street end of Stamford Station. In 1887 the number of trains operating each way out of Stamford Station was thirty. In 1907 the track between New York and Stamford was electrified.

RAILROAD BRIDGE, *c.* 1896. This stone arched bridge spanning the Mill River between Greenwich Avenue and South Street was erected in 1847. It was later reinforced.

IRON RAILROAD BRIDGE, *c.* 1907. A new iron railroad bridge was built just north of the old stone bridge. The Stamford Station can be seen in the background.

ADAMS EXPRESS, c.1900. When the train arrived at the railroad station, the Adams Express Company was there to pick up freight and baggage. By 1919 the same area was lined with taxicabs.

GLENBROOK DEPOT, 1892. Levi Slauson was the ticket agent and the Glenbrook postmaster.

Nine
Worthy of Mention

HOYT FAMILY GATHERING, June 21–22, 1866. Shown is the Hoyt family gathered in front of the Congregational church on Atlantic Street. The Hoyts, among the earliest settlers of Stamford, decided to hold a family reunion. Descendants from New Hampshire to Pennsylvania were invited. As a result of this gathering a family genealogy was published by D.W. Hoyt.

BLIZZARD OF 1888, ATLANTIC SQUARE. One of the worst snowfalls on record was the Blizzard of '88, March 11–14. Three feet of snow fell on the city, closing schools and businesses and suspending railroad and trolley service. The children knew how to take good advantage of the situation.

BLIZZARD OF 1888, MAIN STREET. Another view shows the north side of Main Street after the snowfall. The twin towers belong to the Union House. The snow was so high in front of it, a tunnel was dug to get from the street to the hotel.

GROVER CLEVELAND CAMPAIGN, 1892. At the same time Stamford was celebrating its 250th anniversary, Grover Cleveland was campaigning for president. A political banner is strung across Main Street at the Stamford House. The banner reads, "For Pres. Grover Cleveland of N.Y. / For V.P. Adlai E. Stevenson of Illinois."

GROVER CLEVELAND CAMPAIGN TOUR, 1892. During his tour, Grover Cleveland posed with the men of the Luther Fire Station. Chief Bowman is standing at center between Grover Cleveland (left) and Edward J. Tupper (wearing Derby Hat). To the left of Cleveland is Harry Parker, who became fire chief in 1903.

BUFFALO BILL'S CIRCUS PARADE, May 24, 1898. Indians are circling in Atlantic Square. Circus parades were a popular diversion of the time and the townspeople always turned out in large numbers.

RINGLING BROTHERS CIRCUS, May 20, 1913. The camel team is just entering Atlantic Square from Main Street. The parade was photographed from a window in the Town Hall by Flora May Downing, who held various secretarial positions with the Board of Education until her retirement in the late 1950s.

DECORATION DAY PARADE, 1898. Marching from the west on Main Street toward Atlantic Street, next to the ladies on bicycles, are the members of the Tomesso Campanella Society, led by Lelio Donatelli (in front of flags). This was the first Italian organization in Stamford. Organized in 1894, it was devoted to the general welfare and education of local Italian immigrants.

CIRCUS PARADE, 1905. The parade is on Main Street approaching Atlantic Square from the west. The frame buildings are the Minor Block. To the left from just behind the wagon is Siegelbaum's, then Samuel Price Groceries, and Edwin S. Webb Dry Goods.

SETTLER'S DAY CELEBRATION, 1914. The Stamford Historical Society is credited with pinpointing Settler's Day as May 16. The society designed the city flag and seal. The flag was presented to the city on May 16, 1914, and the seal was presented on April 12, 1916.

STAMFORD CITY SEAL. The ship on the top represents the journey the settlers made across the sea. Moving clockwise from top left, the coat of arms is from Stamford, England; the settler and the Indian were the original Stamfordites; the keys honor Yale & Towne, Stamford's largest industry; and the gristmill was Stamford's first industry. The seal was designed by the historical society.

TEDDY ROOSEVELT VISITS STAMFORD, 1917. On October 12, 1917, former President Teddy Roosevelt visited Jackie Cooper's Health Farm on High Ridge Road to reduce his waistline. He is pictured here (at center) with Chief of Police William Brennan.

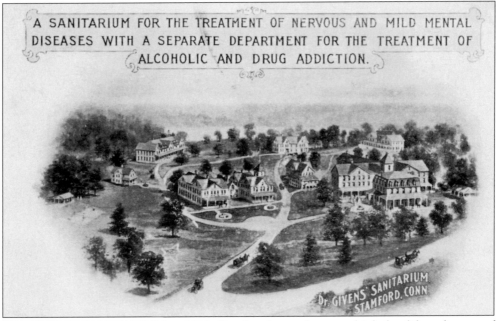

A SANITARIUM FOR THE TREATMENT OF NERVOUS AND MILD MENTAL DISEASES WITH A SEPARATE DEPARTMENT FOR THE TREATMENT OF ALCOHOLIC AND DRUG ADDICTION.

Dr. GIVENS' SANITARIUM STAMFORD, CONN.

DR. GIVEN'S SANITARIUM, c. 1912. One has the tendency to think that life at the turn of the century was free from today's pressures and pitfalls, but such is not the case, as this advertising postcard shows. Dr. Given's Sanitarium was located on Long Ridge just north of Bull's Head. He first came to Stamford in 1892 and established a clinic on Summer Street.

GUTZON BORGLUM STUDIO, *c.* 1900. Sculptor Gutzon Borglum, most remembered for sculpting Mt. Rushmore, had a home and studio on Wire Mill Road. In the photograph with him is his young assistant and model, Bill Arnow. Borglum was a friend of Teddy Roosevelt and played an active role in local politics.

STAMFORD THEATER WITH BORGLUM SCULPTURE, *c.* 1915. The theater opened in 1914. It was built by Emily Wakeman Hartley for legitimate plays. The sculpture over the entrance was designed by Gutzon Borglum and inspired by Eleanora Duse, a popular dancer of the early 1900s.

DANTOWN—REZO WATERS' BASKET SHOP, *c.* 1900. Shown is Rezo at the pounding wheel and son Ernest, at the tub. Rallo, another son, made clam baskets which he took to Fulton Market in New York by horse and wagon. From 1850 to 1900, Dantown, located in North Stamford near New Canaan and Pound Ridge, was a bustling basket center. By 1880 some eighty families were involved in basketweaving and the trade was so important the baskets were used as legal tender in an area of 50 square miles. The business declined in the early 1900s. In 1923, to ensure the city's water supply, a dam was built across the Rippowam River and the Dantown area was flooded, creating Laurel Reservoir.

HAROLD S. LYNN AND HIS GLIDER, October 15, 1910. Harold S. Lynn built and flew this glider on October 15, 1910. He did have a ground crew and flight was "in tow." But, still . . . it's amazing!

ROCK RIMMON ROCK, 1906. This immense boulder, about 60 feet high, is located in North Stamford just south of the junction of Rock Rimmon and Briar Brae Roads. It was at one time a tourist attraction. It has archeological significance as an early Native American rock shelter and was excavated in 1975 and 1980. Native American points and tools were found.

Ten

Private Lives

GILLESPIE CHILDREN, 1890. At their summer cottage at Silver Beach, Shippan Point, are, from left to right, George, Hilliard, Meryl, Edna, and Edward.

GILLESPIES AT SILVER BEACH, 1888. The Gillespies relax on the porch of their cottage at Silver Beach, Shippan Point. The boy in the front is holding a very long bamboo fishing pole. The Gillespie family owned and operated the *Advocate* for many years.

C.O. MILLER FAMILY, THANKSGIVING DAY, 1904. Posing on the front porch of the C.O. Miller home at 48 South Street are, at back from left, Cousin Will, C.O. Miller, and Hannie Miller; on the railing is Carrie; and in front from left are Gladys, Sara, and Charlie. Sara and Charlie are the children of Hannie and C.O. Miller.

WATERBURY HOME ON SCOFIELDTOWN RD., *c.* 1895–1905. Members of the Waterbury, Scofield, and Strohmeyers families have gathered at the Waterbury house.

EDWIN S. HOLLY HOUSE, MAIN STREET, *c.* 1898. This house, built in the eighteenth century, stood on Main Street in the vicinity of the present Central Fire Station. This is the south side of Main between Greyrock and Elm Street.

GOTHIC HOUSE, *c*. 1892. This house was built by George E. Waring at Broad and Bedford Streets. Waring was the owner of Stamford Stove Foundry. For a time his factory stood just behind the house. The present Ferguson Library stands on this site.

RESIDENCE OF HENRY TOWNE, 1892. This home, known as Rockland, was built by Henry Towne in 1879. He lived in this house at Henry and Atlantic Streets until his sudden departure in 1892. Mr. Towne was the owner of Yale & Towne Manufacturing Co. The home later became Rockland Hotel. The hotel burned in 1970.

RESIDENCE OF DR. H.P. GEIB, 1889. This house was located on Strawberry Hill. It was one of the most scenic parts of town and many fine homes were built here, often by wealthy people from New York City.

RESIDENCE OF JAMES I. RAYMOND, 1889. Also located on Strawberry Hill was this fine home built in 1886. It is still standing, but has been divided into apartments. The address is now Hackett Circle, which is entered from Strawberry Hill. Raymond was an importer of oriental wares. His firm was located in New York City.

TAYLOR-VAIL HOME, 1892. Even the houses got all decked out for the 250th anniversary of Stamford. This handsome home stood at Main and South Streets facing Rippowam Park from 1888 to 1921. It was built by Presbyterian Minister Richard Vail and later owned by W.H. Taylor.

WARDWELL HOME, c. 1900. This was the home of Dr. Franklin Wardwell and was located at 585 Elm Street opposite St. Mary's Church. It was built by Silas Scofield in 1850 and was demolished in 1957.

HOME OF JARVIS WEED, *c.* 1900. This home is located at 149 Weed Avenue overlooking Cove Pond. It is in a severe state of disrepair.

HOME OF MRS. EDWARD G. SMITH, RICHMOND HILL, 1890.

HOME OF MRS. ANNA B. TIMOTHY, *c.* 1900. This house is located at the corner of Erskine and Old Long Ridge Roads.

MAYAPPLE FARMS, *c.* 1900. This photograph shows apple pickers on the North Stamford farm.

PONY RIDES — CLARK'S HILL, *c.* 1912. One of the simple pleasures of the time for children was having the "Pony Man" come down the street and offer pony rides for 25¢. Often the ride included getting your picture taken.

JOHN VOSGERAU AND FAMILY, 1916. This is a picture of German immigrant John Vosgerau and his family in front of their home at 22 Winthrop Lane.

SPELKE BASEBALL TEAM, 1905. Baseball was popular, as were other sports, at the turn of the century. This private team was managed by Abraham Spelke (top left). Team members, from left to right, are: (front row) O'Keefe, "Spider" Rabinowitz, and Mascot Burke; (middle row) Donnelly, Sauter, Nichols, and Smith; (back row) Hoyt, Cuddy, Smith, and Howard.

BICYCLE CLUB, 1892. The bicycle club is posed at the old Wire Mill on Wire Mill Road. At center is Mrs. Amy Peckam, wife of Dr. Ellery Peckham. In the 1890s bicycle riding was a popular pastime and there were several wheel clubs.

SUBURBAN CLUB, *c.* 1893. This is the former residence of George A. Hoyt, who built an entire area south of the railroad tracks known as Hoytville. Located on Main Street and Greyrock Place, this house was built in the 1860s. Mr. Hoyt lived there until his death in 1887. The Suburban Club was organized in 1890 and rented Mr. Hoyt's home in 1893. The club built and moved to its own building at Suburban Avenue and Main Street in 1914, where it remained until it was forced to close in 1935. Its demise was blamed on the development of the automobile and the rural country club.

STAMFORD RIFLE CLUB, c. 1906. The club was incorporated in 1902 and had a clubhouse in Long Ridge, at the end of what is now called Gun Club Road, off Erskine. The names of the men trap shooting are Haviland, Gedney, Ball, Preston Jones, Joe Jessup, and Clarence June.

STAMFORD RIFLE CLUB, 1908. This photograph shows the men eating watermelon outside the second cabin (the first cabin burned in 1900). They are on the eastern slope of the Mianus Gorge.